A Picture Book of CWM

A Village near the town of Ebbw Vale, Gwent
(Home of the 1992 Garden Festival)

Volume 2

by Margaret Blackwell

Foreword by
Fred Read

Old Bakehouse Publications

Abertillery

First published in June 2001

ISBN 1 874538 92 1

Published in the U.K. by
Old Bakehouse Publications
Church Street,
Abertillery, Gwent NP13 1EA
Telephone: 01495 212600 Fax: 01495 216222
www.mediamaster.co.uk/oldbakebooks

Made and printed in the UK
by J.R. Davies (Printers) Ltd.

Foreword

by

Fred Read

After accepting Margaret's invitation to write the foreword to her second book of photographs of Cwm, I began to get 'cold feet'. Here I am, an 'Abertillerian' introducing a photographic panoply of Cwm. On reflection I realised I am now a naturalised member of the community of Cwm. I lived in Abertillery for twenty-four years but have now resided at 36 Bailey Street, Cwm for forty-seven years.

During this time I have been involved in the education and leisure time activities of the young people from four-year olds in the nursery class at Cwm Primary School to sixteen-year olds at Dyffryn Secondary Modern and on to eighteen-year olds in Cwm Community Youth Centre. Added to this was my involvement with the Presbyterian Church (now closed and where I was married in July 1953) and now Tirzah Baptist Church.

I sit back and remember the activities of the Dyffryn Choir and my close friend and teaching associate Mr. Patrick Sheen, who to me is synonymous with Cwm, the Dyffryn Youth Club's Youth Soccer Team winning the North Mon. Youth League and cup on their first season in this competition. I think also of Sunday School anniversaries at the Presbyterian under the guidance of Mr. Douglas Cool and so many more wonderful memories.

I was a member of the organising committee of Cwm carnival from its inception when the floats, up to forty in number and often ten jazz bands paraded through the streets of Cwm, followed up by so many events at the field including of course the 'Mountain Climb'.

The production of *Oliver* at the Parish Hall brought home to me the superb team spirit of this community. So much help appeared from all quarters - emergency lighting provided by the Marine Colliery - miners' lamps charged up each day and an immediate coupling of the chairs in rows - timber and cord provided by E.V.U.D.C. organised by Councillor Fred Bird. Then the taking of the whole production to the Beaufort Theatre in aid of Councillor Roy Edmunds' appeal when he was chairman of the council. I have in my possession a copy of Charles Dickens' *Oliver* with a foreword written by Roy.

I could fill a book with wonderful memories of the kind-hearted, community-minded and supportive people (my kind of people) of Cwm. This second book of photographs compiled by Margaret will provide you with your own personal memories of people, places and events of 'Our Community'.

Contents

Introduction

When 'A Picture Book of Cwm' was first published in November 1997 little did I realise the warm and widespread reception that a book portraying our community would receive, an event that subsequently required two reprints. Whilst neighbouring Ebbw Vale has received attention through numerous books and publications over the years, it has been gratifying to myself and I'm sure to many more, that our village of Cwm has eventually received similar consideration. It was a great credit that so many local inhabitants came forward with photographs from their personal collections to help compile that first book and now, yet again they have offered much more material to be included in this second volume for which I am very grateful.

The history of Cwm does of course, go back further than the renowned Marine Colliery, a name that once epitomised the village and attracted an influx of workers to the area, thereby creating a unique community. Iron was smelted here during the latter years of the eighteenth century, the ore itself being transported from Ebbw Vale via a tramroad, this ancient route being used for the foundations of the Great Western Railway Company when they opened their lines through the valley in 1852.

By the brook in front of Cendl Terrace is a flat piece of ground and it was here that the iron ore was processed into metal ingots. These ingots were then loaded onto trams just outside the Crown Inn, later to be known as Crown House and transported to Crumlin from where they were transferred to canal barges for the journey to Newport. The lack of oak trees on the mountainside of Cwm is particularly attributed to their felling during the iron years and the necessary charcoal-making.

There are a number of names that may sound familiar to local residents such as James Snelling who built the Coliseum cinema and also part of Canning Street. It was he who put the name to Crosscombe Terrace, so-called after the village where he was born in Somerset. Then there was the Coombes family, local undertakers and carpenters who were also involved in the construction of the terrace. The Coombes were also responsible for the building of the original wooden War Memorial which stood in Cwm for many years. A name that was inadvertently omitted from the first book was that of Samuel Harbin, who was the town crier until he fell victim to the colliery disaster in 1927 and I am grateful to a living relative who brought the matter to my attention.

Again, my sincere thanks are extended to everyone who loaned photographs for this publication although, due to the numbers received and limited space, some unfortunately have had to be saved for another day.

Margaret Blackwell

CHAPTER 1

Scenes of Cwm

1. An early view overlooking the village of Cwm that dates from the very early 1900s with much development yet to take place.

2. During the early years of the twentieth century, Station Terrace, was a principal shopping street in Cwm. Today it has a purely residential appearance but, with plans afoot for the new road through the area, it is very likely that this part of the village will alter considerably.

3. An early photograph of the village which was taken before the Market Hall was built; also to be noted is that the houses of William Street have been constructed right down to the road. In later years the first three or four houses in William Street were pulled down when they became unsafe due to subsidence.

4. In the twenty-first century the role of the Post Office throughout the country is under scrutiny and a subject of much debate. This was not so when this picture was taken in 1901 of Cwm's office in Station Terrace, a sub-office of Ebbw Vale. Most of the local finances were transacted through the office which at the time was in the capable hands of sub-postmaster Mr. David Stephens. Other names that might be remembered are Mrs. Williams who ran the office in Marine Street and Mr. Davies who ran it in Mill Terrace for a number of years and Mr. Doug Chislett who was postmaster from 1951 to 1982.

5. A different view of Cwm towards the rear of the new Police Station looking down to Mill Street Methodist Chapel. This photograph was taken from the Drill Hall Lodge.

6. The Drill Hall which shows the Remembrance Plaque to those who served in the Boer War. This plaque which was fixed above the door of the building was moved to the Cenotaph when the Drill Hall was demolished in 1996.

7. The elegant building named Boot House once occupied by Mrs. James who is seen standing outside one of the entrances. Mrs. James was referred to as the Lady of Cwm in her lifetime, a nickname given by locals after watching her travel to church every Sunday in her horse-drawn carriage. During the war of 1939-1945, Boot House was to become the residence of three separate families in the period of evacuation and housing shortage.

8. Another picture of some buildings from the village's past that have since been demolished. This is the old Fire Station which was opposite the Parish Hall and in the background can be seen the gentlemen's toilet and the station goods yard.

9. A crowd is gathered in Oak Street sometime during 1948 to view some extensive fire damage. What started as a blaze contained at Number 14, soon spread, wrecking an additional two properties as seen here.

10. At the time of this photograph in 1908, the local fire service was of a rather primitive kind as witnessed by this hand-pulled contraption. The picture was taken in Cwm Terrace with Mr. L. Coombes sat on the ladder with Mr. J. G. Coombes just behind. This 'ancient' fire appliance was made by Mr. L. Coombes.

11. The period has now advanced to the year 1916 and the Cwm Fire Brigade proudly poses with its latest acquisition, a fully motorised fire engine. Sat in the front and wearing a brass helmet is Captain Lazarus Coombes who is immediately behind Mr. R.Williams (The Bailey Arms). Also seen in the picture are Mr. Pritchard (The Victoria Arms), Mr. J. G. Coombes and Mr. C. Coombes.

12. A 1950s photograph that depicts the rural scenery available in the Cwm area. Below, in the Ebbw Valley, can be seen the Aberbeeg road and the landscape is as it appeared before the Forestry Commission commenced the transformation to today's appearance.

13. A general view that was probably photographed during the late 1930s shows features such as Chapel House (the old Primitive Methodist) and the stack belonging to the colliery.

14. A more modern general view of Cwm and it will be noticed that a small industrial site has now been built where Dyffryn School once stood.

15./16. In the upper photograph may be seen some once-familiar places of worship such as the Baptist, Wesleyan and Presbyterian chapels. In the picture below are some scenes of Marine Street, Crosscombe Terrace and Station Terrace; also in view are the Castle Inn and shop.

17./18. Two more views from the mountainside that illustrate the numerous streets and buildings of Cwm. The picture above shows Stanfield Street, Marine Street and Railway Terrace whilst the lower photograph is a general view taken from the east.

19. A picture that emanates from the latter half of the nineteenth century shows the lower part of Railway View. Nestling at the foot of the mountain and to the left can be seen Tirzah Chapel; early evidence of industrial activity is provided by the old coal-level in the background.

20. A view of not too many years ago, yet there are many buildings that are no longer standing such as the Coliseum, Institute, Workmen's Club, Café and Ambulance Hall, Police Station, Drill Hall, Goods Yard, Crown House, Cwm Top School, Golding's Stables and Shop, Bailey's Stables and Boot House. Also to be noted are some roofs that have been repaired with patchwork tiles following the memorable winter of 1947.

21. The Garden Festival became a national attraction in the area in 1992 and this picture illustrates some of the necessary changes that affected the local scenery. Behind the football fields in the distance are the tips at the lower end of the steelworks and the house in Park Gardens, all subsequently removed for the Festival site.

22. Cemetery Road facing towards Waunlwyd as it looked some forty years before this book was published. Through the trees on the left are the once-familiar waste tips and the mountain Domen Fawr.

23./24. Two overviews of Cwm from the early 1950s that will further stimulate readers' memories. In the foreground of the picture above, is Clyde Williams's bakehouse and centre left is the Presbyterian Chapel next to the Institute. In the picture below are excellent views of Dyffryn Infants' School, Dyffryn Villas and Railway Terrace.

25. In the left foreground are the Primitive Methodist Chapel and Boot House (The Old Boot) on land since redeveloped with the building of pensioners' bungalows. In the centre is the Presbyterian Chapel with an unusual white roof; this was a temporary asbestos addition following the winter damage of 1947.

26. The town in later years which shows Cwmyrdderch Court, the flats having been constructed in the mid 1970s.

27./28. Some camera-work from December 1971 provides these two photographs showing Golding's buildings and the canteen belonging to the Infants' School on the left; to the right are Brighton Terrace and School Terrace.

29./30. The Garden Festival of 1992 necessitated numerous local improvements and here are two pictures from Marine Street, looking in both directions whilst housing refurbishment is in progress.

31./32. Centrally in the upper photograph is Cwmyrdderch (Top) School when it was surrounded by green fields; whilst below, the same school has now been accompanied by Curre Street and Canning Street.

33. Most villages have one and this a scene entitled 'Lovers Lane, Cwm'. From the 1960s, the picture captures mountain ponies looking above Cemetery Road in the direction of the Festival site.

34. Whilst this is a more modern view it may well be of historic interest in the not too distant future, pending the construction of a new road through the district which might well change the scene. In this picture is seen the Health Centre, where once stood the Coliseum Cinema and the flats, formerly the site of the school.

35. Crown House was once a familiar and ancient landmark in Cwm. It was originally built as a public house in the late eighteenth century, to be known as the Crown Inn and following closure as a licensed premises, it was to serve a number of uses. In complete contrast, it was to become the first meeting place for pupils of St. Paul's Church Sunday School and later again, the surgery and home of Dr. Mackintosh. In ensuing years the building changed hands and remained as a private residence until final demolition in the 1970s.

36. Here is another very old dwelling place, the last house still remaining at Llandafal which is now in a state of disrepair and presently used to house animals; in the background can be seen Waterloo Terrace.

37. Memorials relating to the Boer War in South Africa (1900-1902) are few and far between these days, however there is one to be seen in Cwm. Originally situated in the Drill Hall, the commemorative stone was re-located in October 1997 to be placed adjacent to the cenotaph. The occasion was marked by a procession through the village and a service led by a contingent of the 3. Royal Regiment of Wales.

38. A rear view of the 'new' Institute which replaced the original Workmen's Institute in 1995, the old building having served the community for almost 80 years.

39./40. A final opportunity to see another of the village's former buildings before and after the demolition programme. Above, in 1995, the café and ambulance hall are boarded up in readiness and below, in 1997, this is all that remains.

41./42. A further example of the changing face of Cwm is witnessed by the disappearance of the Workingmen's Club which stood in Crosscombe Terrace. Above, the building is seen in a boarded-up and sorry state awaiting demolition, whilst below, it has now been razed to the ground leaving a familiar empty space.

43. A 1920s view of the village, much of which has since disappeared. In the foreground are River Row, the Presbyterian Chapel, The Institute, Co-op and Crown Buildings. The large building centre left is the Coliseum and there are good views of Goldings buildings and stables. This photograph pre-dates the building of Emlyn Road and the top end of Cendl Terrace.

44. Station Terrace as it appeared during the 1930s showing the since-demolished Ambulance Hall next door to the Baptist Chapel. As may be seen by the design of some of the windows, there were several shops here at one time, the area being the main street for shopping before Marine Street was developed. To confirm this, one of the houses recently renovated still had the butcher's hook attached to the wall.

45. One last look at Station Terrace from some ninety years ago, the picture having been taken further down the road than the previous photograph and now showing the collection of shops that once occupied this part of Cwm.

46. Now one of the busiest road junctions in the town, this picture taken opposite the old Co-op building in about 1959, illustrates well just how much the traffic has increased over the years. It is still the hope that a much-needed by-pass will help restore normality.

47. The final picture in this first chapter is a rural one from the 1940s and shows the former double-tracked railway lines that ran between Aberbeeg and Ebbw Vale.

CHAPTER 2

People & Events

48. Members of the local Police Force, Fire Brigade and British Legion are on parade here during the 1940s, possibly a Remembrance Parade led by a Mayoral car.

49. A photograph that confirms traffic problems caused by the volume of commercial vehicles passing through Cwm are nothing new. This is the scene outside the Post Office in about 1965 when a heavy truck caused some unexpected chaos.

50. As evidenced by the previous picture, the Post Office was out of action for a short while and the unusual step was taken to open temporary premises in the garage at the side of the building. Postmaster Doug Chislett is accompanied by the ladies Mrs. Dix, Wendy Price, Dawn Chaplin-Lewis and Sheila Brown.

51. Torrential rain in December 1979 caused widespread flooding in the Ebbw Valley and this was the scene on the road between the colliery and Dyffryn School. The water was obviously deep enough for a local canoeist to get some practice in.

52. The following few photographs illustrate some instances of the effects of inclement weather when it hits Cwm. This is a scene from the winter of 1947 when numerous valleys in south Wales ground to a halt; the queue for bread and provisions is seen stretching some way around the corner of the former Co-op Store.

53. Another photograph of a long queue outside the Co-op in Canning Street in 1947. This patiently waiting queue starts outside the butchery door and, as this was a period of substantial rationing following the war, the fact that food could not be delivered because of the weather, was the 'last straw' for many!

54. The days of 1947 continue with this photograph of some local gentlemen volunteers attempting to clear the bridge. Notice that at this time the bridge was quite narrow and had timber-built sides.

55./56. Both road and rail traffic came to a standstill when snowfalls and drifts reached record levels. Here are two views of the station when some bids were made to clear part of the line. Below, some railway staff and members of the public take a rare opportunity to trespass on the track!

57. This is a wintry view of the mountains looking down into Cwm and the photograph was taken from the site now totally occupied by the Festival Park shopping complex.

58. Another scene of damage in the streets of the village, this time caused by extreme weather. The truck has skidded backwards from the steep bridge, fortunately only demolishing an old type wooden lamppost, the year is again 1947.

59. Road marking in the village is in progress by the old fashioned method of manual painting. The period is the 1940s and with no type of modern machinery available, the task was very laborious; in the background Emlyn Road is to be seen.

60. More mature residents of Cwm will remember not only the winter of 1947 but also, the Griffin Bus Company's garage at the bottom of Newcombe Terrace. This unusual winter scene pictures a few stray sheep gathered in the garage seeking shelter from the elements.

61. One sure way of keeping the home fires burning during fuel shortages in winter was to collect one's own coal supply from the nearest colliery. These local men are pictured hauling a sledgefull from the Marine Pit in 1947.

62. During the 1939/1945 War an essential organisation throughout the country was the Home Guard, a voluntary part-time military force for the defence of the realm. Seen here is a platoon of Cwm men on the march through Aberbeeg and apparently being inspected on the right by an American officer. Notice the car's headlamps which have been virtually 'blacked out' for night driving.

63. Another picture of some of the village's military representation in years gone by, members of the Territorial Army. Unfortunately it has not been possible to trace their names on this occasion other than Mr. Charles Ricketts who is sat on the extreme right.

64. The year 1926 is still best remembered as the year of the 'General Strike' when industry and transport throughout the country were brought to a halt for some eight days in support of the miners. There were immediate scarcities and with local mines at a standstill for many months, poverty reigned. Here is a typical mobile kitchen provided by the Salvation Army in Cwm and the lady holding the teapot is Mrs. Gaydon.

65. Sat in the landau is Mrs. James of Boot House and the two gentlemen in top hats are her sons Taliesyn and Abel whose duties were to care for the horses and carriage and convey their mother wherever needed, in this early mode of transport around Cwm. The occasion seen here is to celebrate the Investiture of the Prince of Wales (Prince Edward - later King Edward VIII) in 1911. The girl dressed as 'Britannia' is Flossie Coombes and the picture, taken by Cwm photographer Mr. D.J. Draper, includes several local veterans of the Boer War.

66. Susan Jeffrey and Daniel Davies are seen in action at Cwm Merddog, an area of ancient woodland that receives the care and attention of the Gwent Wildlife Trust. Planned nature conservation by generous volunteers is intended to restore, maintain and improve the land to its natural habitat providing interesting country for walkers and wildlife.

67. The two major employers for Cwm residents in past years were Marine Colliery and Richard Thomas and Baldwin's (RTB's) steelworks at nearby Ebbw Vale. An annual event eagerly awaited was the pantomime performed at the Palace Cinema Ebbw Vale and this picture shows the children of Cwm boarding the bus outside the Institute in about 1950.

68. Another local bus trip, this time enjoyed by the ladies of Cwm and a few youngsters. The date is uncertain but included in the photograph are Pearl James and Rosie George.

69. Cutting the cake are Doctor and Mrs. Mazin outside the vicarage in 1973, the occasion being to mark the ninetieth anniversary of the opening of St. Pauls Church.

70. Two gentlemen stood at the lower end of Railway View and on the right is Mr. William Lewis Farr who was born and bred at the Mill Farm in 1873, later to become the local blacksmith.

71. From the late 1940s is this picture of some local scout campers which includes Brian Rees, Dennis Freebury, Mary and Marlene Henry, Mrs. Banfield and P. Griffiths.

72. The St. John Ambulance Brigade was started in Cwm in 1913 and this picture shows some local enthusiasts at an award presentation in 1984; the Deputy Assistant Commissioner Mrs. V. Wilmot is seen surrounded by some nursing cadets in Mill Terrace Church schoolroom. Certificates were presented to Nicola Evans, Rachel Stead, Catherine Gough, Angelina Jones, Patricia Peek, Catherine Phillips with Junior certificates going to Rebecca Stead and Claire Lewis.

73. Another crowd of young ladies, the Brownies, pose for a photograph during the 1960s and most of the names have been given as follows. Back row: Karen Robbins, Hazel Griffiths, Ms. Davies, Susan May, Beverly Jones, Judith Day, Christine Gould, Lyn Bennett, Jill Lewis, Eleanor Forrest, Leigh Clarke, Julie and Siân Evans. Front: Paula Roper, Judith Bennett, Sharon Davies, Carolyn Phillips, Janice Farr, Lesley Bayliss, Diane Bryant and Gail Warren.

74./75. Armistice Day has been marked every year (usually the nearest Sunday to November 11th) since the end of World War One in 1918. Here are two pictures of a Cwm parade in the 1950s with the Boys' Brigade bringing up the rear - the group including Cliff Shaw, Tom Phillips and Alan May. At the head of the same parade is the Salvation Army band leading the way.

76. Some of the biggest street parties everywhere were held in the summer of 1945 to celebrate the end of six years of war. This is the scene in Marine Street from that period and amongst the many partygoers are Mrs. Grist, Mrs. Challenger and Pam Prescott.

77. Margaret Clark (Baloo) is seen here supervising a group of Cubs and Brownies to a special service held in St. Paul's Church.

78./79. Two photographs that illustrate the popularity of the Scout and Girl Guides movement that once prevailed in the district. The upper picture with a huge local gathering is from the 1920s whilst below, the group is from the 1940s and the scout master is Mr. Cliff Henry.

80. From the 1950s a summer camp is enjoyed by the local scout group and seen relaxing here for a moment are Cliff Henry, Vicar Jones and Boss Banfield.

81. The 'Boys Brigade' was a very popular institution in years gone by and here are members of the Cwm group. They are pictured at the side of the Congregational Chapel in Marine Street and somewhere in the photograph, Cyril Green and Tom Phillips are to be seen.

82. The girls and their leaders parade past some former familiar advertising hoardings which stood near the Baileys Arms back in 1969. At the front is Carolyn Forrest in front of Elsie Lewis and Glenys Bayliss with Janice Farr carrying the standard. Amongst the other youngsters are Sharon Childs and Susan Taylor.

83. Cwm Town Band, who had the distinction of appearing on nationwide BBC Radio in 1937. The band with their conductor, display a number of cups on the large drum and the picture was taken at the back of the Institute where the fire wardens headquarters were built during the 1939-45 War.

84. A local band of a different variety was that led by Mr. Pope. This popular group was well known in the district during the 1920s and 1930s, frequently to be seen performing at local concerts and dances.

85. Another scene from the 1920s, possibly a chorus line from a local pantomime and the troupe includes the following ladies Hetty Morgan, Daisy Parsons, Clara Thomas, Dot Campbell, Eva Rees, Violet Price, Freda Small, Gwen Medland and Maggie Driscoll.

86. More local entertainers are seen here with a variety of wind and stringed instruments who form the Waunlwyd and Cwm Orchestral Society. Many of the names are known, a few belonging to the same family apparently and reading from left to right, included are Ambrose Pope, Walter Brewer, Tom Bayliss, William Jenkins, Edwin Gould, William Brewer, William Rogers, John Roberts (Bandmaster), Jack Rose, Frank Rose, Harry Cray, Alfred Pope, William Jones, John Pope, Messrs. Jones, Palmer, Palmer and Tommy (Gee) Edwards.

87. From the 1930s, when stage shows were a most popular form of entertainment comes this group of artistes which includes Haydn Pope, Tom Smith and Ivor Smith.

88. Cwm Male Voice Choir and accompanying artistes in 1969 includes the following - Back: Bill Price, Len Brain, Tom Gronnow, Fred Hayter, Dennis O'Brian, Ken Button, and Roy Carpenter. Third row: Rees Owen, Bill Pritchard, Ron Thomas, Ernie Watkins, Stan Plummer and Bill Edwards. Second Row: Ron Farr, Nurse ?, George Marsh, Norman Evans, Dick Smith, Russ Butcher, Stan Gatehouse, Les Evans, Josh Williams and Bill Sayce. Front: Stan Davies (Conductor), Mr. Edwards (Colliery Manager) and his wife, Joyce Smith (Artiste), Maureen Day (Pianist) and Nancy Harwood (Artiste).

89. Members and honoured guests are seen here in this photograph of the Cwm Male Voice Choir which was taken in 1994.

90. This scene from the late 1940s or early 1950s is captioned 'The Wauncwm Male Voice' with Mr. Stan Davies as the conductor.

91. It is not quite certain where or when this picture was taken but the photographer was Mr. Ricketts who used to run his little business from 102 Curre Street. The gentlemen he photographed here are all members of the Cwm Buff Lodge.

92. Whilst this picture is a little worn, there should be be some local grand or great-grandparents to be seen here. The group consists of members of the National Club in Canning Street and the year is about 1924. One gentleman who has been identified is Mr. Alf Nutt who is in the back row, second from the left.

93. Again from the 1920s, comes this group of smartly dressed gentlemen who are members of the Waunlwyd Nibs Outing Club. It's not certain what the overall function of the club was but, such things as a day's trip to the races for instance in a charabanc, in those days, would have been quite an occasion. Some faces to look for include Fred Webber, Cyrus Wiltshire, Syl Clark, Harry Hicks and Jim Lewis.

94. Members of the 'Special Police' who were assisting in the keeping of law and order in Cwm during the 1939-45 War. A strong contingent of twenty-two officers and constables are seen outside the old police station in Falcon Terrace and amongst the force are PC Davies, A. May, Ted Parsons, PC Owen, Fred Willis, R. Draper, Sgt. Hundrel, Tommy Watkins, O. Barnfield (the barber), J.J. Thomas (draper) and Bill Price (Rhondda).

95. These ladies belong to the Townswomen's Guild who are on a day trip along the River Thames. Looking at their head attire, the fashion suggests a period during the 1940s and amongst the crowd are Mrs. Mazin, Mrs. Samuels, Mrs. Workman, Mrs. Evans, Mrs. Coombes, Mrs. G. Hill, Mrs. Sheen, Miss Lloyd and Mrs. E. J. Lunn.

96. A special outing that was held for locals to visit London for the first time after the war and readers may remember a few of the trippers seen here such as Mrs. Perkins, Mrs. Vernon, Mrs. Leonard, Mrs. Carrie Williams, Cyril Moore, Edna Leonard, Mrs. Smith, Mrs. Jones, Mrs. Poultney, Malcolm Evans, Beryl Leonard and Bert Evans.

97. A firm favourite for very many years has been an organised trip to Blackpool and this is a local crowd pictured there in 1954. Amidst the many are Hubert Thomas, John Davies, John Powell, Elvet Poultney, Colin Thomas, Maxwell Hughes, Malcolm Thomas, Doug Harris, Ken Williams, Val Bowden, Mr. and Mrs. Bowden, Mr. and Mrs. Dobbs and Stan Evans.

98. Another popular venue for a little holiday or a day trip is Porthcawl, and here are some Cwm pensioners posing for a photographer during the 1950s. Standing are Ted Parsons, Mrs. Parsons, Mrs. Evans, Hilda Hodson, Mrs. E. Russell, Mrs. Evans, Mrs. Evelyn Thomas, Mrs. Hancock, Mr. Evans and Mrs. Crew. In the front are Alf Hodson, Mrs. L. Grist, Mrs. Barwell, Mrs. Biles, Mrs. E. Challenger and Mrs. E. Smith.

99. A 1960 visit to Blackpool and the photograph consisting mainly of ladies includes Mrs. Price, Mrs. Virgo, Mr. Ingerson, Mr. and Mrs. Samuels, Mrs. Gummer, Mrs. Ruddock, Mr. and Mrs. Wallis, Mr. and Mrs. Meredith, Mrs. Thomas, Mrs. Russell, Mrs. Wicks, Mrs. Cantello, Mrs. Owens, Miss Tuck, Mr. and Mrs. Bird and Mr. and Mrs. Parsons.

100. June 2nd 1953 and this is a crowd from Canning Street celebrating the Coronation, and amongst the residents are Mr. Macey, David Pitman, Dilys Thomas, Barbara Russell, Aeleen Dallimore, Dorothy Williams, Derek Purnell, John Price, Sandra Burgess, Merle Price, Francis Sewell, Jennifer Davies, Judy George, Shirley Carpenter, Rosie George, Jennifer Hill, Jane Dixon, Mary Crees, the MaClean sisters and Victoria Saunders.

101. Members of the St. John Ambulance Brigade pose for an important picture whilst celebrating their winning of the NCB Shield some fifty years ago. Most of their names are known as follows: Back - Mr. Shillabear, H. Brown, G. Griffiths, ? , Jack Price, Tom White, Mr. Williams and W. Price. Front: Mr. Brooks, Richard Simpson, Dr. Pryce Jones, Mr. H. Lee, Mr. E. Moss and Tom Watkins.

102. Another picture of the Brigade which was taken outside the Ambulance Hall during the late 1940s or early 1950s. Seen here are - Back: Bill Farmer and Win Price. Front: Jack Price, Idris Williams, Edgar Moss and George Griffiths.

103./104. Two photographs in this chapter that provide further evidence of the latter-day popularity of the Scout Movement in the village. Above, Brian Rees and Malcolm Brooks are to be seen and below, Mr. Cliff Henry is pictured whilst in charge of a contingent of scouts and cubs.

105. Many local chaps are to be recognized here in the grounds of the Versailles Palace, France in the 1950s. The photograph was taken during one of the trips to Paris when members of the Conservative Club attended a rugby international.

RIVERSIDE SOCIAL CLUB & INSTITUTE.

THE OFFICIAL OPENING OF THE NEW PREMISES AT THE

OLD LUCANIA BILLIARD HALL.

will take place on

Saturday Evening, FEB. 18th 1950

the Opening Ceremony will be performed by
MAJOR. T. H. VILE, of Newport, supported by
W. D. REES, Managing Director of Lloyd's, Newport, Ltd.
Councillor A. THOMAS, J.P.   Chairman E.V.U.D.C.
County Councillor, W. C. MACEY, J.P.

Chairman :- F. WOOLDRIDGE, Esq.

Reception at 6. p.m
Opening Ceremony at 6-30. p. m.

F. A. JOSEPH, Secretary.

CHAPTER 3

Trade & Industrial Workings

106. Mr. and Mrs. Sheppard are stood in the doorway of their general store at number 198 Marine Street during the 1930s.

107. Long before chain supermarkets, most towns had their local Co-op Store which could provide almost anything, there being little need to travel out of town. This photograph was taken inside Cwm's Co-op in the late 1950s, (days when such essentials as biscuits, sugar and butter were sold loose and not pre-packed as we would expect today). The staff seen left to right are Eileen Sainsbury, Gordon Moss (manager), Norma Williams, Marlene Davies, Val Aubrey and Ryd Griffiths.

108. Various members of staff and locals outside Cwm's first Co-op store which stood in School Terrace. Notably on display in the window, is a large stock of tinned fruit, an accompanying notice stating that there are 10,000 large tins of delicious pears available at 7d (3p) a tin.

109. The former Co-op building is now seen as 'The Happy Shopper' and is photographed from the ground left vacant after the demolition of the Institute in 1993. Note the top corner of the building still bears the original 'Provident Society Ltd.' an alternative name for a Co-operative Society.

110. Another popular retailer from the past was Sallis's shop and members of staff are pictured here about seventy years ago. Included in the photograph are Joyce Bailey (4th from the right) and Enid Michael (2nd from the right).

111. Marine Colliery, the sinking of which began in 1887, is pictured here in about 1919 at the height of its production.

112. A much earlier look at the colliery, possibly the early 1890s, as the cottage on the far left of the picture was obscured from view by 1896 with the building of a new signal box to serve the additional railway lines then being constructed.

113. Marine during the 1930s with its two familiar shafts, the second completed for production in 1893. These were quite sizeable for the period, being 18 feet in diameter and reaching a depth of 418 yards.

114. Many of the general office staff at the colliery in 1946 are also accompanied by some fellow tradesmen. Some of those in the picture are J.G. Coombes, Frank Wiggel, Cliff Henry, Bernard Brown, Bert Babbs, Tom White, C. Wyburn, Horace Duncan, R. Simpson (kneeling), J. James (blacksmith) and R.H.S. Davies (electrician on the far right).

115. A group of the colliery's engineers pause for a photograph when the second aerial ropeway was being built. Left to right are Horace Duncan, Frank Griffiths, John Coombes, Needham Evans, Dai Stead and Jim Bayliss.

116./117. Two more views illustrating the extent of the colliery workings during the 1920s and 1930s, the upper photograph showing the road to Aberbeeg. The mine was originally opened and owned by the Ebbw Vale Steel, Iron and Coal Company.

118. Teams of rescuers and ambulances stand by following the tragic accident at Marine on March 1st 1927 which claimed the lives of 52 miners. Unfortunately the name of Mr. Samuel Harbin was omitted from the original published list of casualties causing confusion with the total numbers. He was the town crier and has a descendant still residing in Cwm.

119. Horsedrawn hearses carry some victims of the disaster up the hill towards their final resting place on March 11th 1927.

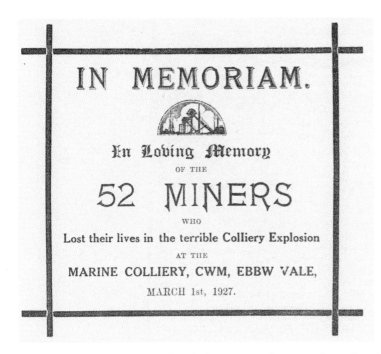

IN MEMORIAM.

In Loving Memory

OF THE

52 MINERS

WHO

Lost their lives in the terrible Colliery Explosion

AT THE

MARINE COLLIERY, CWM, EBBW VALE,

MARCH 1st, 1927.

Saint David's Day 1927 was the most un-celebrated occasion in the history of Cwm and the whole of Wales. This was the day when a total of 52 miners lost their lives in an underground explosion, making it the principality's worst mining accident since the Sengenhydd disaster of 1913. By the time the Marine tragedy was accounted for, the record books showed that a total of 3508 men had been killed in the coal industry in Wales.

The death toll might easily have been much much worse had it not been for the fact that of the 1400 workforce, only some 135 men of the night shift were underground at the time. Surface workers were made aware of an obvious mishap when clouds of smoke suddenly began to pour out of one of the shafts, from a depth of more than 300 metres and the alarm bells were sounded. The first reaction was to alert the mines rescue station at Crumlin who immediately sent teams of their experienced men and summoned the assistance of a number of doctors to the scene.

When no contact could be made through the surface to pit bottom signalling system, it was decided to lower a cage down the shaft not knowing what the risks or results might be. Two men with horrific burns, but still alive, were soon brought to the surface and it was then realised that a massive explosion had taken place and that the damage caused would create great difficulties in mounting a rescue operation. Whilst many volunteers had now reached the scene, because of such dangerous conditions, it was decided that only those with close knowledge of the pit should be allowed to venture to the shaft bottom. Armed with the very latest breathing equipment, it fell upon a traditional method of detecting a presence of gas - a caged canary to assess the situation. As was anticipated, the bird taken to the scene, suffocated amidst the atmosphere of firedamp almost immediately. Apart from the presence of deadly gases, there was enormous damage caused by roof falls and broken machinery all blocking the roadway. Whilst several rescuers were forced to return to the surface, having been overcome by fumes, the mission persevered, a doctor in attendance at all times. Nine badly burned bodies were found fairly quickly with a further twenty, a short distance away, thus suppressing hope of any survivors. The initial explosion was thought to have started in the Black Vein district, confirmed by the fact that those who did survive, told of being at the Old Coal some distance away.

Having worked non-stop for some thirty-six hours, the rescuers and officials declared that 'all hope is abandoned' and a final count showed 52 men dead or missing. Of the 52, 38 were from the village of Cwm itself, the rest coming from Waunlwyd, Ebbw Vale and the Brynmawr district. Canning Street and Marine Street each lost eight of its residents. Funerals were held in Cwm and Ebbw Vale, the Press reporting the largest crowds ever seen in the streets, the processions being led by high ranking officers of the Armed Forces. A number of the victims were buried with full military honours, their coffins draped with the Union Jack and a firing party held by The 3rd Battalion the Monmouthshire Regiment, all in recognition of the years the miners had given to the country in the 1914-18 War. Ironically, on the day of the funeral in Cwm, a bus full of passengers travelling to the occasion crashed through a railings alongside the colliery and overturned, injuring many of the mourners. Local members of the St. John Ambulance Brigade were called away from the sombre ceremony to attend to casualties at the scene.

120. A later scene at Marine just a year or two before its final demise. Financial problems within the Ebbw Vale Company in 1935 brought about the decision to sell its mining operations and Marine was purchased by Partridge, Jones and John Paton Ltd., who already owned another twenty collieries in South Wales. This company ran the Marine successfully until nationalisation in 1947.

121. A somewhat poignant picture that illustrates a gentleman worker at Marine and two of his faithful employees. The importance of the horse to many collieries in the past should not be underestimated, particularly for their haulage capacity. In many instances the animals would be worked, stabled and fed underground and brought to the surface only for a two-week respite during the tradional miners' holidays. This practice, nowadays sounding unkindly, was in operation in many pits around the country until the early 1970s.

122. A graphic picture taken when the colliery finally saw the end of its working life with the wheels and winding gear tumbling to the ground during the demolition in 1990.

123. Miners having completed their shift are seen awaiting the 'colliers train' as it pulls into the halt in the 1950s. The platform and the signal box on the left were built specifically to serve the Marine in 1901.

South Wales Marchers' Organising Council.

SOUTH WALES MINERS'
MARCH to LONDON

CALL TO ACTION! VOLUNTEERS WANTED!

Arising out of the pronouncement by A. J. COOK, 18/9/27, a Miners' March to London from S. Wales is being organised. The March will commence on the day Parliament opens--Nov. 8th, and the Marchers will arrive in London on Nov. 20th, where they will be received by an All London Working Class Demonstration.

The object of the March shall be two-fold, to arouse a Nation-wide feeling concerning the Appalling Conditions in the Mine-fields created by the policy of the Government and the Coal-owners, and to seek an interview with the Prime Minister, the Minister of Mines, the Minister of Labour, and the Minister of Health.

124. One of the few Marine relics remaining on display near the village is the Cornish pump engine, which has been preserved on the site of the former colliery. When in operation, this pump was capable of dealing with 50,000 gallons of water per hour from beneath the ground. Despite a quite gradual, but nationwide run-down of the coal industry which began in the early 1980s, British Coal was still confidently predicting a bright future for the Marine and its 500 or so workers. In 1982 a new coal-winding improvement scheme was implemented at a cost of some two and a half million pounds and things suddenly looked encouraging. This high-speed automated winding system could easily raise more than half a million tonnes of coal per year. In addition, a completely new coal handling plant was installed on the surface. By now, Marine had also been linked to Six Bells colliery near Abertillery, and continued to receive and process the output from that pit until its closure in 1987.

Without much doubt, the prolonged miners' strike of 1984 hastened the political decisions concerning the coal industry and the gradual run-down turned into a torrent. Thus the confidence previously placed in the Marine was short-lived, and although it survived all of its neighbouring working pits, it was eventually closed by British Coal in March 1989.

125./126. Two final views of the colliery that well-illustrate the changes to the environment since pit-closure, both photographs having been taken from the same spot; the workings have been flattened and a new road has been constructed.

127. The Ebbw Valley was once rich with seams of coal, the main ones being Old Coal, Big Vein and Black Vein. As well as the Marine, there were numerous smaller mines dug into the mountainside such as the one seen above, which worked the eastern side of the valley and was known as the Red Ash Level.

128. An essential worker underground until the 1960s and even later at some collieries, was the faithful horse. The blacksmith's job in those days was an important one, keeping the animals hooves in good order. Here is a busy scene from the blacksmiths' shop at Ebbw Vale steelworks with Gilbert Denmead on the far right.

129. In the background of this picture can be seen the Aberbeeg Road and a chimney stack belonging to one of the old coal levels. The gentlemen here, photographed some eighty years ago, are workers from the Marine and include Mr. Joe Sheen who is on the front right.

130. Aneurin Bevan served as MP for Ebbw Vale and Tredegar for 31 years until his untimely death in 1960. Regarded as founder and architect of the NHS, he was of mining stock and could often be seen and heard at local events. He is pictured here after addressing a miners' rally in the Coliseum Cwm during the 1950s.

An Extract From The Memoirs Of A Former Marine Worker

Mining is such a hazardous occupation, safety is always a priority. Regular checks for gas are made but even so, accidents happen. I was eight years of age and innocent of life underground when my childish play was interrupted by the hooters and whistles of the pit and the shrieks of the ambulance sirens. I knew in my inexperienced mind that something dreadful had happened. I remember the date so well, March 1st, 1927 because it was on this same day that my brother William, serving with the 14/20 Hussars at Aldershot died of meningitis.

My friend George Millwater (later to be interned in Colditz) and I ran up to No.1 where we learned that there had been an explosion underground killing 52 men. I was there when the first body, Bob Preston was brought out. Casualties in those days were laid in a four-wheel cart with handles and covered in blankets with just the face in view. Bob was taken to the first house in Marine Street. Another victim was the town crier Sam Harbin and I remember that at his funeral there was a wreath in the shape of a bell. Only two men were brought out alive, both badly gassed and shook up; one of these, Tony Tarr had had presence of mind to put his mouth over an air pipe and avoided the deadly gas.

Many families were bereaved and in one family a father and two sons were killed. I remember the pungent aroma of eucalyptus as the rescuers applied liberal doses to their clothes to overcome the rancid smell of death below. Such a disaster attracted wide publicity and a visit by the Prime Minister of the day Stanley Baldwin was considered a necessary balm for the wounded community. He went to the pit-head and talked to the bereaved families and during the course of his visit I was run over by his car! I didn't wait to see if the great man was concerned for my well-being because I ran away as fast as my legs could carry me - obviously unhurt. Normality after such a disaster was a long time coming and although men were naturally afraid to go back to work underground, lack of other employment and a need to feed families were big factors in resuming work. Six years later at the age of fourteen I started work at the Marine myself, putting the memory of the explosion behind me.

Idris Harwood

131. Back in the 1980s a diesel-hauled train is pictured making its way from Ebbw Vale steelworks. A familiar sight on the left is the former low and narrow bridge, the spot nowadays completely altered.

132./133. The two final photographs in this chapter may be of interest to former railway men in Cwm. Above a mini disaster has occurred during the 1920s on the line to Ebbw Vale but it is not known of any casualties. The lower picture was taken some thirty years later, still in the steam era when gangers are laying some track.

CHAPTER 4

Religious Matters

134. Reverend Basil Williams with his wife and family are seen relaxing for a photograph on the vicarage lawn.

135. A 'confirmation class' in the doorway of St. Paul's during the 1940s is headed by Rev. Basil Williams and the Bishop of Monmouth. Also to be seen are Nurse Hudson, Jean Hudson, Mrs. Thomas, Jean Rogers, Cynthia Hughes, Hazel Cosgrove, Peggy Griffiths, Marlene Henry, Janet Lunn, Mary Henry and Anita Jenkins.

136. St. Paul's Mission Sunday School in Marine Street in about 1948-49 and the pupils include - Back: Shirley Watkinson, Violet Sanderson, Janet Holloway, Marie Gaydon, Margaret Blanchard, Jean Powell and Dennis Jones. Middle: Clifford Watkinson, Billy Nutt, Kenneth Mitchard, Mary Mitchard, Lance Edwards, Sheila Mitchard, Glyn Edwards and Peter Davies. Front: Dylis Powell, David Nutt, Marlene Mitchard, Philip Powell and Janet Woods.

137. The ladies and boys march in song in about 1948. Amongst the faces to be seen are Mrs. Read, Mrs. Hill, Rene Wickson, Mrs. Warlock, Mrs. Workman, Mrs. Dorothy Farr, Mrs. Pritchard, Mrs. Lunn, Mrs. Gill, Janet Lunn, Zelda Walding, John Price and John Mitchard.

138. The choristers receive their certificates and medalions from the Associated Board of Church Music in about 1996. To be seen are Delyn Jones, ?, Irene Hodges, Lindy Wyburn, Louise Price, Kirsty Jones, Ron Farr, Father Brian Ireson, Sandy Ireson, Lauren Jones and Susan Garrett.

St. Paul's Church, Cwm, Ebbw Vale, Monmouthshire,

OPENED FOR DIVINE SERVICE, JULY 5TH, 1882.

ASSETS.	£ s. d.	£ s. d.
Proceeds of Bazaar and Goods subsequently sold	298 5 7½	
Less Expenses	30 19 3	
		267 6 4½
Grants :—		
*Incorporated Church Building Society	100 0 0	
Llandaff Church Extension Society	50 0 0	
		150 0 0
Collections :—		
At the Laying of the Corner Stone	6 17 0	
Cwm Collecting Cards ...	5 7 3	
	12 4 3	
At the Opening Services ...	21 1 6	
		33 5 9
Subscriptions		1,017 13 7
Interest on Money deposited		38 14 2
Balance paid by the Rev. W. Hughes ...		33 9 6½

* This Grant is withheld till the Church is consecrated.

COST OF BUILDING, &c.	£ s. d.	£ s. d.
Fencing and preparing Ground, &c. :—		
West & Son, Fencing North and East Sides of Enclosure	21 0 0	
David Pugh, Fencing South and part of West Sides of Enclosure, and Excavating area of Church ...	95 12 0	
W. Jones & Son, Retaining Wall, &c.	46 10 0	
,, Front Wall, Gate, Pillars, &c.	56 19 2	
Ebbw Vale Co., Coping Bricks, &c.	4 14 2	
Coalbrook Dale Co., Two Sets of Entrance Gates	8 9 3	
T. Jenkins, Hauling Coping Bricks, Red Ashes, &c.	2 2 3	
Labour in levelling Ground, forming Paths, &c.	8 16 10	
Sutton & Sons, Lawn Seeds ...	0 12 6	
		244 16 4
W. Jones & Son, Contract for Building Church	897 0 0	
W. Jones & Son, Extras sanctioned by Architect	205 12 6	
		1,102 12 6
Extra for Glazing East Window (Mr. Norton)		5 10 0
Musgrave & Co., Stove		17 0 0
Mr. J. Norton, Architects		60 0 0
J. Newcombe, Clerk of the Works ...		10 0 0
Furnishing Church :—		
Service Books	2 8 3	
Door Mat	1 3 0	
Wippell & Co.	13 6 6	
Jones & Willis	15 4 4	
W. Jones & Son	14 17 0	
,, Lamps, Pulpit Lights, Platform, &c.	15 9 6	
		62 8 7
Advertising, Printing, Stationery, Postage, &c.		13 0 0
Conveyance of Site :—		
White Borrett, & Co.	12 10 0	
Gabb & Walford	12 12 0	
		25 2 0

£1,540 9 5   £1,540 9 5

139. St. Paul's Girls' Friendly Society with Rev. D.J. Sproule and Mrs. Sproule. Amongst the members are Hilda Davies, Grace Manning, Maisie Wright, Miss Sullivan, Doris Williams, Hilda Noyes and a very young John Sproule.

140. St. Paul's Parish Hall is the venue for this play group, the period being the 1980s.

141. Hopefully there are a few recognisable faces here belonging to St. Paul's Church choir who are seen here during a visit to Tintern Abbey in 1951. Among the choristers are R. Smith, R.F. Lunn, H.J. Lunn and S. Gill.

142. Coronation celebrations in June 1953 are in progress by the Mothers' Union at St. Paul's and faces to look out for include Mrs. Carter, Mrs. Gill, Mrs. Price, Mrs. Hill, Mrs. Workman, Mrs. Phillips, Mrs. Warlock, Mrs. Read, Mrs. Williams, Mrs. Miles, Mrs. Noyes, Mrs. Ivy Hill, Mrs. Pritchard, Mrs. Farr, Mrs. Pembridge, Mrs. Thomas, Mrs. Crees, Mrs. Purnell, Mrs. Abraham, Mrs. Alford and Mrs. Lunn.

143. An incident in December 1991 brought some alarm to the pupils and teachers inside Mill Street Methodist Chapel who were busy rehearsing their Christmas concert. A lorry failed to climb Cwm bridge and ran backwards into the chapel, causing considerable damage to the frontage as seen in this photograph.

144. Golden Jubilee celebrations were held at Mill Street Methodist in July 1973, with the dedication of a new organ being the predominant event. Mrs. Mills is sat at the keyboard and amongst the onlookers are Phyllis Pitman, Mrs. Edwards, Mrs. Watkins, Mrs. Price, Mr. Mills, Mr. Sayce and daughter, Mrs. Virgo, Mrs. Jones, Mrs. Sayce, Betty Moss and Mrs. Dix.

145. Unfortunately there are too many names to trace on this picture but it is of Cwm's Sunday School Union production of 'Stargazers' in 1982.

146. An early 1930s photograph of the Presbyterian Chapel Choir and reading left to right from the back are Howard Cool, Ivy Sherman, Ivy Moore, Campbell Davies, Quentin Young, Billy Davies, Doll Brennan, Lil Clarke, Stella Price, Hazel and Eileen Hobbs, Elsie Hayter, Melvin Mitchard, the Brennan brothers, Billy Morris, Ben Jenkins, Doug Cool, Gwyneth Cool, Job Cool - conductor, Mary Morris, Rosie Battle, Nancy Gilbert, Enid Rendle, Gwyneth Samuels, Thelma Woods and Mary Morris.

147. Another picture of some members of the Presbyterians some years later than the previous photograph, the occasion being a chapel turnout in 1952. Amongst the marchers are Beryl and Sylvia Gummer, Gladys Peak, Joyce Farmer, Pam Price, David and Derek Hodges, Sandra Burgess, Rosemary and Annette Taylor and Barbara Smith.

148. A dedicated group of followers of the Salvation Army in Cwm are seen in about 1950 and included are Mr. Carr, G. Fry, Mr. Darby, Mr. Edwards, Mr. Reeves, Mrs. Gaydon, Mrs. Fry, Mr. Probert, Mrs. Easter, Mrs. Phelps, Mrs A .Edwards and Mrs. D. Llewellyn.

149. Some younger members of the corps and their leaders during a walkabout in the village probably during the early 1950s. Mrs. Phelps and Mrs. Probert look on but the only other names which have come to light are Judy George and the Tranter sisters.

150./151. Two further pictures that illustrate the strength and popularity of the Salvation Army movement in the village. Above is probably a Whitsun march through Marine Street and below, members are seen posed for a photograph outside their headquarters at the top of Stanfield Street.

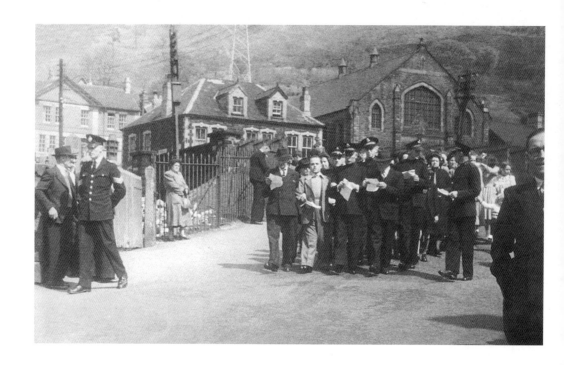

152./153. The final photographs of the Salvation Army supporters are of marchers who are in full song coming down from the bridge, and below, the ladies and children are parading past the Co-op building during the 1950s.

154. In the traditional style, gentlemen link arms to lead a procession with ladies close behind, all members of the Baptist Chapel during the period 1945-46. The scene is in Curre Street and at the helm is Reverend B. P. Pritchard who is accompanied by conductor Mr. Stanley Amos.

155. Some more familiar faces to be seen inside Tirzah Baptist Chapel are - Back: Ron Selfe, A. Watkins, Mr. R. Lewis, Mr. B. Lewis, Mr. H. Mitchard and Mr. W. A. Price. Front: Fred Sharpe, Mrs. and Reverend R. Evans, Mrs. M. Hendy and Mr. D. Jones.

156. The retirement of Mr. Charles Pitts, a long-serving superintendent of Tirzah Sunday School is acknowledged here by a presentation of a fine barometer and the fellow officers looking on include Danny Thomas, Nancy Stacey, Fred Sharpe, Edna Price, Doris Probert, Charles Pitts, Beryl Jones, Rev. W.J. Evans, Ron Selfe and Ron Lewis.

157./158. Two scenes from more than eighty years ago when an unexplained fire destroyed Tirzah Baptist Church causing great distress to the worshippers. However, they were a most determined gathering and not to be beaten, soon organized groups of local volunteers, a number of whom are seen here ready to begin the re-building.

159.   Various members of the Sunday School Union are pictured here for a celebratory tea held in the Wesleyan Methodist schoolroom sometime in the 1950s. Stood at the back are Mel Williams, Mrs. Gullick, Mrs. Gardner, Mrs. Llewellyn, Mrs. Rose, Miss Clara Thomas, Mrs. Sprague, Mrs. Pritchard, Mr. and Mrs. Gillett. Seated at the table are Marion Williams, Mrs. Williams, the Salvation Army captain, Mr. Trembath, Mr. Williams, Mrs. Trembath, County Councillor Florrie Morgan and Reg Morgan.

160.   All of Cwm's religious organizations would have been proud to parade through the streets in years gone by and in this picture from the early 1950s, it is the turn of the Primitive Methodist with the familiar face of Mr. Carpenter to be seen in the front row.

161./162. Now almost 120 years old and having stood the test of time, the imposing church of St. Paul's is seen from an unusual angle. Close by is the vicarage and on the extreme right may be seen the old stables belonging to the Bailey Arms. The photograph below shows the interior of the church with its east-facing windows as it looked about 75 years ago with its ornate lighting. When completed in July 1882 this parish church had cost an enormous sum for the period of £1540.

163. Some more young people on the march that includes Ann Pembridge, Ann Watson, Diane Courts, Coral White, Marie Gaydon, Charles Wall, Ann and Gaynor Williams, Mrs. Morgan Jones, Ann Tapper, Jan Denmead, Jean Powell, Miss Jones, Margaret Wall, Shirley Watkinson and Diane Coombes.

164. This march photographed in about 1950 includes Arthur Williams and his brother, Mr. Kinsbury, Ivor Hill, Harry Workman, Dick Smith, Billy Read (Mission House), Mr. Walding and Cliff Henry.

CHAPTER 5

Schooldays

165. This would have been a treasured document to any school pupil, including proud parents and teachers in the 'good old days'. The certificate, portraying members of the Royal Family, was presented to Mabel Baker of Dyffryn Girls School who by July 1917, had achieved the maximum possible school attendances of 404 out of 404, a feat that would take some challenging these days.

166. Dyffryn 'New School' is pictured meeting its demise at the hands of a Caterpillar earth mover. This particular block contained a number of essential educational centres such as two kitchens for the cookery pupils (a skill reserved for girls only in times past), a metalwork room and woodwork room. Former pupils may also remember the upper floor containing a laboratory whilst the grounds were appropriately used for gardening.

167. This is how the expansive Dyffryn School appeared in this unique photograph which dates from the year 1913.

168. Younger readers may wonder a little at this photograph which illustrates what the interior of a school in Cwm looked like ninety years ago. It is of Dyffryn school and is more than likely the assembly hall.

169./170. Two distinctive school photographs from the Dyffryn of 1913 that more than anything illustrate the type of uniforms that were required in those days. Whilst it is almost impossible to identify anyone here, the lower picture of Standard 1 does contain John Davies in the centre and, sixth from the left, in the second row from the front is Russell Butcher.

171./172. Two final photographs of the scene at Dyffryn in 1913. Above are members of staff of the boys and girls departments and at the time Mr. Edward Boore was headmaster and Miss James was in charge of the girls. Below, the boys are all from Standard 3.

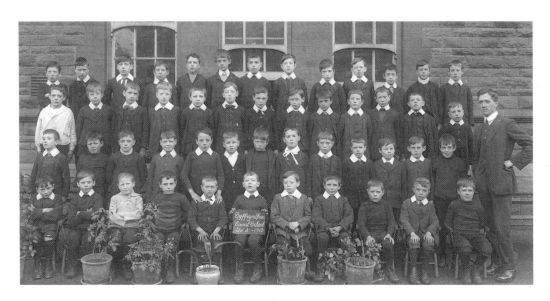

173. The date is August 1958 and one of celebration as the Dyffryn School Choir were victors in the under 16s childrens' choirs at the National Eisteddfod held in Ebbw Vale. In the picture are Susan Davies, Marilyn Lewis, Marilyn Williams, Pam Gronnow, Zelda Dalimore, Pam Carpenter, Jill Kirby, Carol Brooks, Brenda Noyes, Barbara Russell, Delyn Williams, Marilyn Jones, Bernice West, Jean Tovey, Beryl Harwood and Francis Selfe.

174. A photograph that was taken in the yard at the 'Top Infants' School in the 1950s and here are some faces to look out for. Back: Miss Bullen, Delwyn Baker, Roy Saunders, John Morris, Alan Weeks, ?, Glyn Jones (doctor's son), Gaynor Williams, Marilyn Williams, Colin Griffiths, ?, Billy George, Brian Edmunds, Peter Gill, Miss Williams. Front: Mary Bush, Elunid Rees, Mary Crees, Gaynor Graydon, Jennifer Court, Iris Langdon, Pat Gummer, Judith George, Annette Taylor, Jeanette Easterbrook, ?, Dorothy Jones.

175. Cwm 'Top School' in 1952 and hopefully there are a few boys and girls to be remembered. In the back are Ernie Gerrish, Ken Lewis, Norman Hole, David Hodges, Alan Grist (sadly killed at Ebbw Vale steelworks in later years), Derek Hodges, Gwyn Marshall and teacher Miss Williams. Front: Jennifer Hill, Janice Gummer, Janice Hendy, Pat Dix, Andrea Turvey, Linda Harris, Gaynor Lewis, Susan Robinson, Joan Blanchard and headmistress Mrs. James.

176. A class of 1948-49 at the school and whilst it has not been possible to put a name to all of the pupils, there are a few who have been traced reading from left to right. Front: Les Cross, Malcolm Nurden, Ken Moores, Reg Talbot, Mr. Lewis, Ann Jones, Marie Gaydon, Dilys Gaydon, Marion Watson and Sylvia Jones. At the front are Dorothy Brennan, Trevor Barnes, Ray Dicks, Mervyn Robins, Brian Gillett, Alan Davies, Marlene Lewis, Val Bowden, Ann Probert and Glenda Watkins. Back: David Harris, ?, ?, Barry Evans, ?, ?, John Williams, Brian Whitcombe, Phillip Gill, Cyril Robbins and Eric Carpenter.

177. Some more local youngsters are posing for the camera here in the 1950s and standing are Norman Taylor, Vernon Tranter, Billy Lewis, Melvin Harris, John Garrett, Malcolm Lewis, John Wallace, Vincent Avery, Roy Saunders and Billy Jenkins. Kneeling: Evelyn Nutt, Shirley Preece, Margaret Jones, Moira Gillett and Aeleen Dallimore. Seated: Shirley Troake, Veronica Compton, Doreen Dunster, Elaine Watkins, June Parsons, Pat Warfield, Elaine Jenkins, Anita Jones, Ann Pembridge, Cyril Robins, David Ross and David Edwards.

178. Cwmyrdderch School in about 1925 and the teacher in the centre is Mr. Tom Jenkins. Mr. Jenkins' pupils include the following - Back: Messrs. Lewis, Matthews, Rupert ?, Williams, Grist, Moss, Crees, Prosser, Powell, Pitts, E. Yates, Moore, Stephenson and Forbes. 4th Row: Misses Medland, Ricketts, Jean ?, Moore, Taylor, Day, Dallimore, Gwen ?, Dallimore and Jenkins. 3rd Row: Misses Bigglestone, Norde, Booton, Crees, Pritchard, Wright, Pratten, Wilcox, ?, Veater, Hill and Pugh. 2nd Row: Misses Taylor, Pitts, Gulliver, ?, Taylor, Strickland, Mr. Jenkins, Prosser, - the rest unidentified. Front: H. Rogers, Norman Michael, W. Evans, J. Price, R. Okley, L. Evans and J. C. Coombes (later to be killed in action).

179. This time its the turn of some members of staff at Cwmyrdderch to be pictured in the 1950s. In the back row are Messers Powell, Lunn, Craig, Evans, Orchard, Lewis and Thomas (apologies to the unknown). Front: Miss Knapton, Miss Morris, Mr. Williams (headmaster), Mrs. Williams and Miss Harris.

180. Although this photograph comes from the years 1905-06, there may well be a few readers who will recognize a grandparent or two. In the bottom left hand corner are Mabel Baker and Amy Williams and in the back row is Tom Rule.

181. Some infants at Cwm New School, Class 6, are dressed for an apparent St. David's Day celebration in 1981. These infants would now be adults in their mid-twenties at the time of publication of this book and here are a few names to look out for. Back: Steven Shaw, Dafydd Hemmings, Neil Jones, Darren Price, Ross Davies, (last two unknown unfortunately). Middle: Tania Harris, Katie McAndrews, Melanie Tranter, Nicola Pope, Louise Williams, Denise Holmes, Charmaine Spellman, Sharon Wyatt and Sarah Jane Smith. Front: Hugh Jenkins, Philip Marshall and Mark Whyatt.

182. The date is July 1st 1959 and teacher Mr. David Hughes is seen with some of his pupils who are - Back: Francis Spinetti, Terry Blanchard, Brian Jones, Brian Clegg, John White, Philip Williams, Allan Hawkins, John Holvey and David Lewis. 3rd Row: Susan Evans, Brenda Shaw, Pat Mills, M. Griffiths, Sheila Penaluna, D. Price, Maureen Barnes, S. May and M. Smart. 2nd Row: C. Dobbs, M. Adams, P .Harris, A. Hayter, Pat Fry, Jane Bull and Ann Button. Front: David Parfitt, Malcolm Werry, M. Dallimore, C. Fear, D. Warren, Linda Crees, Keren Edmunds and Clive Hill.

183. Some more pupils from the Top School and this is how they all looked in the year 1958. In the back are Lyndon Matthews, Paul Timothy, Jeff Davies, David Henry, Michael Atwood and Philip Jenkins. 3rd Row: Nancy Wilkinson, Jennifer Penaluna, Mary Crees, Aurddolen Williams, Penny Stephens, Frances Selfe, Pat Jones, Suzanne Sayce and Ann Clark. 2nd Row: Susan Burgess, Gail Price, Susan Harvey, Lorraine Harrington, Julie Lewis, Gillian Davies and Sheila Poultney. Front: Michael Llewellyn, Alan Williams, Colin Williamson and John Hooper.

184. In about 1958 teacher Pat Smith is accompanied by some boys and girls. Reading from left to right, starting at the back the names given are Robert Moore, Henry Spinetti, John Alford, Terry Poultney, Martin Bruton, Peter Cahill, Susan Tunley, Marie Woodyatt, Iris Williams, Sheryl Woods, Elaine Alden, Sylvia Shaw, Irene Francis, Irene Jukes, Marion Wareham, Angela Harris, Lesley May, Carol Parsons, Ann Thomas, Colin Jones, Leighton Pitman.

185. In the yard at the top school, this time during the 1950s and most of the names are available for recognition as follows. Back: Stanley Robbins, Dale Prior, Colin Owen, Granville Williams, Charles Wall, Neil Sheen, Ken Brookman, John Tucker, Derek Carpenter. Middle: Denise Kirby, Marlene Ashman, Doreen Pitman, Yvonne Williams. Front: Dawn Parfitt, Pat Morgan, Delyn Williams, Ann Bull, Louise Antoniazzi, ? , Jean Thomas, Rosemary Lewis, Beryl Harwood, Lana Sims.

186. Teachers and pupils at Cwm New School are seen here in 1978 and the list of names is as follows. Back: Miss Poole, Jason Gunter, Christopher Williams, Michael Sayce, Sean Meyrick, Derek Rowlands, Tony Jones, Christopher Burns, Andrew Bird and Mr. Lewis. 3rd Row: Jason Morgan, Howell Williams, Amanda Pope, Rachel Stead, Joanna Evans, Tracy Weeks, Nicola Wilcox, Stephen Robins and Mark Lewis. 2nd Row: Julie Saunders, Kerry Prosser, Debbie Stanley, Nicola Evans, Donna Courts, Patricia Peek, Nicola Bull and Tracy King. Front: Andrew Pugh, Damon Evans, Neil Jones and Neville Rossiter.

187. Not all of the names have been traced for this school picture but on the left, back row is headmaster Mr. Cox and on the far right is teacher Pat Cronin. The school-children are George Humphries, Philip Harris, Simon West, Malcolm Padfield, Richard ?, John or Wayne Harris ?, Neil Wilstead, Geoffrey Smith, Richard Ashman, Carolyn Forrest, Susan Wilcox, Helen Woodland, Deborah Powell, Mandy Prosser, Maria Forrest, Maria Llewellyn, Annette Hewlett, Ian Watkins, Sally ?, Lyn Brown, Linda Woods, Jane Leonard, Deborah Day, Carolyn Farr, Paula Baker, Karen Roper, Ellen Jones, Ian Watkins, Mark Winters, Gareth Jones, Geoffrey Gardner, Anthony ?, Denzil Jones.

An extract from an early history of Cwmyrdderch School - the first 75 years

The first record of the School is in 1876 when, on August 1st, a new Headmaster, James Malson, was appointed. The school was then situated in the old Baptist Schoolroom (bottom Railway View). There were 60 pupils, and the fees were 2d per week. The school was named Cwmyrdderch Board School and the staff during the first year was James Malson (Headmaster), Mrs. Lewis (Sewing Mistress), William Price and Morgan Thomas (paid monitors at £5 per annum).

In April 1879, the school was moved to its present premises, the numbers having risen to 110. There were only two rooms available, yet by 1881 the numbers had risen to 210. In 1882 Lydia Worthing was appointed. Little of event happened until 1883, when the Headmaster was replaced by Mr. J.T. Bedford who was to remain for 36 years. The school was considerably extended. During the 1890s the school was frequently closed through epidemics and bad weather. A local strike caused much hardship, and meals in school were introduced as a temporary measure. In 1900 there were 430 pupils and the staff was J.T. Bedford (Head), Mr. J. Bower, Mr. M. Vickery, Miss Light, Miss Jones, Miss Kay, Miss R. Orchard and Miss J. Williams (Infants).

There were several staff changes, and in 1902 a visiting H.M. Inspector reported the accommodation as inadequate. In November 1904 the Secretary of the Education Committee stressed the need for a new school. The numbers rose to such an extent that Godfrey's Buildings, the Parish Hall, Smith's Buildings and the Baptist and Wesleyan Vestries were all used. The number on the books (including infants) rose to 953 in 1909. In 1911 this was temporarily improved when Dyffryn opened under Mr. E. Boore (August 29th). In February 1912 Mr. Lunn first taught here. In 1913 Fire Drill was instituted and practised during the war. There were now 362 pupils and many of the staff in the Army. Married women taken on. 1916 Staff strike 14 days. At the end of the war there were 384 on roll and girls were now receiving Laundry and Housewifery classes at Willowtown. A good report was given by an inspector in 1920 and in 1921 the school was repainted. There were 200 needy children being given breakfast and dinner. In 1924 Mr. Bedford retired and Mr. Tom Morgan became Headmaster.

There were soon staff changes. Children attended Shakespeare lectures in Ebbw Vale and also a film of the 1924 Wembley Exhibition. The Ebbw Vale swimming baths were first visited in 1933. In 1936 Mr. T. Morgan was replaced by Mr. J. Killey. The school choir had a B.B.C. audition and there was an inspection. Again the report condemned the buildings but stressed good results under bad conditions.

A.R.P. lectures for staff were introduced in 1938 and many of the children were immunised against Diptheria. In 1939 Mr. Killey went to Waunlwyd and Mr. Jack Roberts became Headmaster. In September 1939, the first evacuees came. A school garden was obtained next to the school but one night sheep entered and destroyed 320 cabbages. Shortly after this the garden was leased to some Policemen. In December 1943 Mr. Jack Roberts retired and was replaced by Mr. E. Roberts. Victory Celebrations followed the end of the war in 1945 with teas and other entertainments for the children. In 1947 the school was closed for six weeks due to snow, the conditions being described as the worst within living memory.

In September 1948 Mr. W. Williams took over as Head after the retirement of Mr. Roberts and the school now had a staff of thirteen teachers.

188. This is an up to date picture of the nursery class and we have the names as follows. The Headmaster is Mr. Phillips accompanied by nursery teacher Miss P. Roden on the right and nursery nurse Mrs. L. Evans on the left. The children, left to right are - Back: Grant Davies, Joshua Mitchard, Abigail Timothy, Ieuan Monks, Christian Whittle, Luke McCarthy, Jack Jones and Jack Squibb. Middle: Carys Jones, Kate Dance, Matthew Stevens, Adam Denmead, Jordan Johnson, Beau Davies and Steven Wetten. Front: Lauren Watson, Dafydd Mold, Chad Price, Lucy Fry, Lewis Morgan, Sean Edwards, Bethan Davies and Daryl Davies.

189. Here is a photograph of the victorious boys' soccer team at Dyffryn School displaying the Junior Cup. Tom Morgan the headmaster is on the left and sports master Wilf Jones is on the right. The boys, reading left to right are Vince Harvey, J. Morris, Wilf Rogers, Ted Lawrence, Master Powell, J. Harris, Graham Brookman, Henry Jones, Morris Llewellyn, Roy Cross and J. Morris.

CHAPTER 6
Scenes of Sport and Entertainment

190. The village has of course produced a celebrated snooker champion by way of Mark Williams but here are some players from the Institute a few years back, displaying a shield and cups. A few names have come to light yet local readers may well be able to add a few more but amongst the crowd are Mr. Grist, Mr. Macey, Mr. Smith, Malcolm Thomas, Bert Thomas, Mr. Pitman, Mr. Weeks, Mr. G. Price, Mr. Hudson and Mr. Cross.

191. In many valley towns may be found an ex-servicemen's club and invariably it will be better known as 'The Dug-out', a name brought back from the trenches. Here are members of Cwm's 'Dug-out' skittles team with a trophy probably during the 1920s.

192. Some more skittlers are seen at the National Club in Canning Street probably during the early 1950s and in the centre, front row is to be seen Doug Langdon.

193. An opportunity for a selection of just some of the 'Glamorous Grandmothers' of Cwm to appear in a book eventually, and a few names to remember are Mrs. Langdon, Mrs. Swan, Mrs. Tarr and Mrs. George.

194. Many of the children sat here with their parents, will by now be parents themselves having posed for the camera during a 'Young Wives' outing to Bristol Zoo in about 1966. Left to right may be seen Carolyn Farr, Marion Farr, Janice Farr, Mr. L. Bayliss, Mrs. Glenys Bayliss, Aldyth and Jane Bayliss, Judith and Lynn Bennett and Helen Bayliss.

195. Former secretary of the Riverside Club William John Leary is seen having just received a presentation to mark his retirement and also in the picture are Bert Henry, Larry Kirkham, W.J. Leary, Councillor Harry Evans and Mr. Cyril Herridge.

196. The neighbours of Brook Place and Canning Street are seen celebrating the Coronation in June 1953 and here are but a few of the partygoers - Mr. and Mrs. Sharp, Mr. and Mrs. Chislett, Mr. and Mrs. Butcher, Mr. and Mrs. Stevens, Mr. and Mrs. Rutter, Mr. and Mrs. Cameron, Mr. and Mrs. Shaw and Susan, Mr. and Mrs. Samuels, Mr. and Mrs. Evans, Mr. and Mrs. Harbin, Ginny Long, Mr. and Mrs. Negus, Mrs. Coombes and Mrs. Watkins.

197./198. Two more parties held in the streets of the village. Above, the ladies are feasting in Curre Street and below, Itton Street celebrates the Investiture of the Prince of Wales in 1969. Among those in Itton Street are Bryn Baker, Tom Gronnow, Eric Gibson, Marion Farr, Mrs. Rees, Mrs. Wilcox, Ceinwen Rhead, Mrs. Hillier and John Bennett.

199. In the good old days of the Co-op in Cwm it was customary to hold the occasional dinner and dance and here are some of the staff at such an event in 1955. Left to right are - Val Aubrey, Les Bird, Mary Mitchard, Malcolm Brooks, Dilys Gaydon, Jean Ryan, Noel Baker and Maureen Taylor.

200. Back in the 1950s amongst many forms of entertainment was the production of a pantomime at the Institute and here is the cast of *'Little Red Riding Hood'*. The players seen in some unorthodox attire are Derek Kirby, Keith Mason, Ray Potts, Horace Mitchard, David Quantick and Tom Dance.

201. The majority of Cwm's residents of today, will only recall the parties and celebrations held in the summer of 1995 to mark the fiftieth anniversary of the end of war in Europe. The photograph above is from the original event in May 1945, the party being held in the middle of Elm Street with a three-piece band providing some musical entertainment.

202. Members of Dyffryn School Choir are seen during a German tour, probably during the 1950s and amongst the ensemble are Patrick Sheen (conductor), Pauline Aubrey (accompanist), Miss Richard, Mr. Jones, Sandra Burgess, Dawn Parfitt and Avril Palmer.

203. Many members of the Coombes family are assembled here at Ebbw Vale for a photograph in 1923 and reading left to right, from the back the group includes Charles, John C. and John G. Coombes, Mrs. L, Mr. F. and Nora Coombes. Mrs. E. Lunn, Mrs. N. Evans, Kathleen Coombes, Mrs. F. Goddard, Mr. Lewis, P. Taylor, R.F. Lunn, Eleanor Goddard, Mrs. C. Coombes, Mrs. Lewis. In the foreground are Agnes Coombes and Marjorie Evans.

204. A studio portrait of Mr. Ellis Evans who for many years was the music teacher at Dyffryn School, he leaving there in 1950.

205. Unfortunately it has not been possible to ascertain the names belonging to the many faces seen here during the 1950s or early 1960s but it is confirmed that they are victorious members of Riverside Ladies Skittles Team accompanied by a few gentlemen in the back row.

206. Some more strong-armed ladies belonging to the Riverside Club are seen performing at a club sports day. Included in the tug of war team are Mrs. McDonald, Dot Herridge, Mrs. Blick, Blod Forte and Rosie George.

207. The Parish Hall is the venue for this coronation party organized by the residents of Emlyn Road in June 1953. Faces to look out for include Mrs. Cosgrove, Mrs. Payne, Ivy Baker, George Baker, Daisy Pitman, Mrs. Williams, Iris Rowlands, Lil and Bill Harris, Mr. Harris, Sally Jones and the young lad stood on the left is Granville Williams.

208. A popular sport and form of entertainment at the Riverside was the game of skittles and here are some ladies with a coveted trophy in 1954. Back Row: Mrs. McDonald, Mrs. McDonald, ?, Mrs. Webber. Front: Dorothy Herridge, Pearl James, Gwen Manning, Maisie Wright and Mrs. Swansbury.

209. The Cwm carnival is always a well-attended event and this is a scene from the occasion on August 24th 1985 when Nicola Langdon was the queen. Nicola's court is comprised of Rachel Stead and Carri Prosser at the back, assisted by Lucy Powell, Adelle Guest, Angelina Jones and Denise Holmes.

210. Some members of staff at the old Coliseum Cinema who may be remembered by some readers. Pictured are Bill James, Ambrose James and Lou Lewis. Ambrose was caretaker for a number of years and Lou worked there until closure in 1957.

211. Quite possibly this picture was taken during the Festival of Britain celebrations in 1951, the group being seen at the bottom end of Crosscombe with the Oak Hotel in the background. To be seen are Marjorie Evans, Mary Lunn, Zelda Walding, Janet Lunn and Jean Hudson.

212. Another sporting conqueror from the past was John Wilcox seen here at the age of fourteen whilst living at number 2 Curre Street. Titles came from the Welsh Amateur Boxing Association, seven-stone intermediate, Welsh schoolboys in 1933.

213. Frank Wilcox in carnival dress about 1930. The brook with the iron fencing in the background and the big stone was an area known as the corner, a popular children's play ground.

214. The victors of the Cyrus Davies cup during the 1947-8 season, defeating Tredegar Ironsides 9-0 at Brynmawr. Reading left to right faces to look for are Elliot Penny, George Waggett, Colin Wakely, Ron Cameron, Lyndon Matthews, Fred Rose, Ivor Smith, Aneurin Penny, Bill Morgan, Harry Morgan, Tom Burton, Ben Stibbs, Horace Matthews (capt.), Ray Hall, Tom Jones, Ginger Chaplin, Mr. Grist, George Forward, Norman Darby, Fred Day, Bill Saunders and officers of the Mon. Junior Union.

215. A triumphant soccer team from Dyffryn School with a shield and cup in 1948-9. Back row: J.J. Jones (headmaster), Eric Matthews, Gwynfi Phillips, David Williams, Wilf Jones (sportsmaster) and Mr. Billy Phillips. Middle: Jim Sayce, Ray Denmead, Desmond Holloway, Ken Smallcombe and John Gaydon. Front: Sid Hawkins, John Bennett and John Jones.

216. Cwm RFC in 1955-56 and in the foreground are Mr. Arrowsmith, A. Biles, L. Matthews, A. Forster and C. Lapham. Behind are T. Cameron, Mr. Smith, Mr. Davies, Mr. Baugh, Mr. Powell, Mr. Porter, Mr. Noyes, J. Gaydon, K. Cameron, and J. Virgo.

217. The final photograph in this book goes to the Cwm New School soccer team in the 1970s where most of the lads' names have been found. Back: Stephen Evans, Chris Parfitt, ?, Philip King, Daryl Griffiths, Chris Parsons and Darren Parsons. Front: Julian Price, Justin Price, Michael Watkins, Jeremy Hughes and Delroy Stanley.

Acknowledgements

Acknowledgements are due to the undermentioned who kindly loaned their own photographs for inclusion in this book. Sincere apologies are extended to anyone who may have been inadvertently omitted.

Fred Antell, Gwen Beese, Ivy Brennon, Ann Button, Ken Cameron, Jack Carpenter, Doreen Chislett, Gerald Clark, Sid Clarke, Jack Coombes, Midge Courts, Glenys Davies, Howard Davies, Susan Davies, Hayley Denmead, Stan Dobbs, Elaine Edmunds, Ann Edwards, Margaret Evans, Marion Farr, Dilys Gaydon, Aldwyn Giles, Philip Gill, Eileen Gronnow, Beryl Harris, Val Hayden, Roy Hole, Jean Holmes, Dennis Jones, Margaret Jones, Thelma Lawrence, Pat Luke, Joan May, Granville Moss, Glenys Parfitt, Marlene Parfitt, Roy Parsons, Marion Phillips, Phylis Pitman, Ann Pope, Edith Poultney, Adrian Quantick, Ann Ratcliff, Bill Rose, Mrs. Selfe, Mary Shaw, Bert Smith, Veena Smith, Elaine Thomas, Malcolm Thomas, Ron Thomas, Anita Watkins, Evelyn Webber, Margaret Williams, Lil Williamson, Olwen Wright.
